# Dogs Really Do Talk!

written by
John R. Scannell

illustrated by
Devika Joglekar

Wutherwood Press

For my wonderful grandchildren

Opal, Conway, Walter, Weston, and Eleanor

&

their parents

Mandy & Nick, Becky & Ryan, Ben & Caroline

Conway

Luigi Di'Ogee L'Amour

Viscount Wolfric Wolfie
von Wutherwood

Weston

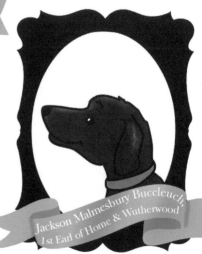

Jackson Malmesbury Buccleuch,
1st Earl of Home & Wutherwood

Hi, my name is Conway, and have I got a story for you.

I'm five years old, and my little brother, Weston, is three. We spent the last two days visiting Grandma Wendy and Grandpa John. Mom and Dad told us it would be like "a trip to the country," and they were right. But it was even better than just "a trip to the country." You'll see.

It was a beautiful summer Seattle day. On the way to Grandma's we drove across the Lake Washington "floating bridge"—that's right, a bridge that floats on Lake Washington just like a boat. As we drove across it, we could see the bright-white, snowy top of Mount Rainier way, way off. It looked like a big ice cream sundae.

Trips to Grandma and Grandpa's house always feel like they take forever, but when we saw the long white fence and all the tall trees, we knew we were there. We laughed and cheered. "We're here! We're here!"

"Okay," said Mom. "We're here. But before Dad and I let you out of the car, I need you to tell me the magic words. Do you remember them?"

I took a moment to whisper to Weston—he's only three—and then the two of us yelled, "Please!"

"Very good," said Dad. "'Please' is the best magic word. But aren't there a few more magic words?"

We both shook our heads 'yes'—big smiles on our faces. "Thank you!" we shouted together.

"Very good. 'Please' and 'thank you' will make your Grandma and Grandpa smile. Being polite is really important," Mom reminded us.

"Very important," said Dad.

"Well, Dad," Mom said, "I think our little boys are growing up—and I think they're ready to say hello to Grandma and Grandpa."

As we opened our car doors, three enthusiastic dogs ran toward us, wagging their tails and barking their greetings.

"Look Conway. Doggies!" laughed Weston. "Doggies!"

"That's right, Weston," Grandma Wendy said as she scooped us up and hugged me and Weston. "Three doggies!" Then she hugged Mom and Dad.

"Three doggies for Conway and Weston," said Grandma. "Boy, are they happy to see you. They've been waiting all morning for you to get here."

"They have?" I asked.

"Yes, they have. We've been telling them how much fun little boys can be. Lots more fun than me or Grandpa, isn't that right, Grandpa?"

"Absolutely," said Grandpa.

"Do you remember their names?" Grandma asked.

Weston got down on one knee and petted the smallest dog who put his paws up on Weston's leg.

"This is Luigi," Weston said as Luigi, a Boston terrier/pug, licked Weston's face.

"And this is Jackson," I said happily. Jackson, a Black Lab/Coon Hound, sat down right in front of me, his long furry tail wagging like crazy. "He's almost as tall as me!"

"And do you remember who this is?" Grandma asked me, pointing to the largest of the dogs. Grandma's Chow Chow sat right beside her, his fluffy red fur gleaming in the sunshine.

"That's Wolfie," I said as I wrapped my arms around Wolfie's fluffy neck.

"That's right," said Grandpa. "Wolfie! He's our Big Dog!"

Wolfie wagged his tail as Grandpa patted his head.

"Now you boys can do whatever you want here," Grandpa told us. "Just stay inside the white fence. You can climb trees, chase the rabbits, eat blackberries..."

I was just so excited. "Weston, we can climb trees, eat berries..."

"Berries? Yum!" laughed Weston. "Can we eat lots of berries?"

"You can eat berries until your bellies explode," Dad said.

Weston pulled up his shirt and showed everyone his belly.

Mom and Dad and Grandma and Grandpa laughed. "Here's some bouncy balls for you guys," Grandpa said, handing each of us our own blue rubber ball. "The dogs will love playing with you."

I squeezed my bouncy ball in my hand, smiled a smile that told Jackson, "I'm gonna throw this ball," and threw it as far as I could toward the apple tree in the middle of the yard.

Jackson bounded after the ball—and so did Luigi. We followed the dogs into the yard, running into the bright August sunshine.

We played fetch for a long time with Jackson and Luigi—Wolfie doesn't play fetch—and then Luigi wanted to lay down in the sunshine for a nap. When Weston and I looked back, we could see Mom and Dad and Grandma and Grandpa on the front deck drinking lemonade.

So Weston and I decided to climb trees. Then we decided to run after the bunny rabbits who scampered everywhere. I mean everywhere. Boy, are they fast! We didn't catch any.

We saw bunches of squirrels, too. And lots and lots of different kinds of birds. Grandma keeps birdfeeders in different places around the garden. We even saw hummingbirds hovering around a hummingbird feeder hanging from a tree branch. Hummingbirds are like helicopters!

Grandma told us, "The birds have to eat, too, Conway, especially in the winter. It's summer now, but when it gets cold, they know where they can get their food."

They sure knew. They flew to and from the feeders all day long. I told Grandma, "Your feeders are just like restaurants for the birds."

She laughed when I said that.

Everyone watched us from the front deck and waved to us whenever we looked their way.

Weston and I were up in an apple tree when we heard a funny noise. A real fast tapping noise.

"What's that noise?" Weston asked. He sounded worried.

We heard it again.

"Grandma," I shouted as I waved my arms. "Grandma, the tree is making a really funny noise."

Grandma came out beneath the apple tree, and she heard it, too. She smiled and asked us if we wanted to see something special.

We said, "Sure," and we swung down from the tree and landed in the soft grass. Grandma led us quietly toward the strange noise.

"Be very quiet and look up there," Grandma said as she pointed up into the branches of the pine tree above the white fence.

Well, we looked, but we couldn't see anything. But we could hear it. It was a funny tapping noise. All of a sudden, a big, red-headed bird came hopping around to our side of the tree. It was hopping and holding onto the tree like he had magnets in his feet.

He hopped, then tapped the tree with his nose, then hopped again.

"That's a red-headed woodpecker," Grandma said. "He's using his beak to look for bugs."

Weston wrinkled his nose, "Bugs?"

"Yep," said Grandma, "that's what he eats. He's looking for dinner."

Weston and I watched with Grandma for a long time. We'd never seen a woodpecker so close, except maybe on TV.

TAP TAP

After we said goodbye to the woodpecker, Mom and Dad said it was time for them to get going home, too.

"Be good," Mom and Dad said. "Don't forget the magic words."

We kissed and hugged Mom and Dad, and waved as they drove off.

Grandma turned to us and said, "You two have been very busy in the yard. I bet you'd enjoy eating some blackberries."

"Til our bellies 'splode?" asked Weston.

"That's right," Grandma said. "But you have to be careful as you pick them. Blackberries bite, you know."

"Berries bite?" asked Weston. "Do they have teeth?"

"Well, not teeth, exactly. These wild blackberries have sharp thorns that you must not touch. Those thorns will bite you if you aren't careful."

"We'll be careful, won't we, Weston?"

"Yep," Weston said. "We'll be careful, Grandma."

"Good. Well, you go ahead and pick some berries. Come on in when you want."

Grandma left us next to the berry patch, and she and Grandpa went into the house.

That's when something amazing happened. Really amazing. Honest to goodness.

"Make sure you remember what your Grandmother said," said a voice behind me.

Weston and I turned around to see who said that. We didn't recognize the kind and gentle voice.

We looked around. We walked toward the apple tree, then toward the fence, then toward the house. No one was there.

"Your Grandmother said to be careful, and I'm here to make sure you are careful," said the same kind, gentle voice.

"Who said that?" I asked, looking around. That's when I was sure someone was playing a trick on us. "Grandpa? Is that you, Grandpa?" I motioned for Weston to look into the tangled stalks of berries.

"Grandpa, are you hiding in the berries?"

"Do I sound like your Grandfather?" asked the voice.

That's when I turned and looked right into Wolfie's face.

Wolfie was sitting about five feet away from me—while Jackson and Luigi rested beneath the apple tree about twenty feet away. Wolfie cocked his head to one side.

"You've never heard a dog talk before?" Wolfie asked us.

I just shook my head. "No. I didn't know dogs could talk," I said.

"Of course dogs can talk," Wolfie said.

"Well, I know you bark, and all, but I mean talk."

"Doesn't this sound like talking, Conway?" Wolfie asked.

"Yes, it does. And you know my name?"

"Of course, I do. And you know my name. Everyone has a name. I know your brother, Weston, too."

I have to say, I didn't know what to think. I'd never heard a dog talk. Not ever. Neither had Weston. Weston and I knelt down in the grass in front of Wolfie.

"Wolfie's talking!" said Weston in a surprised voice.

"Do you talk to Grandma and Grandpa, too?" I asked.

"In a way. Children can understand dog talk better than adults. As humans grow older, they begin to lose their ability to understand dog conversation," Wolfie explained.

"Do Luigi and Jackson talk, too?"

"Of course. Not as well as I do, but they talk. Keep in mind that Jackson is just a young pup."

"What about the cats?" I asked. Grandma and Grandpa had three cats.

"Cats are pretty picky about who they talk to, Conway. They have what we call 'cattitude.' Maybe they'll talk to you and Weston. You'll have to ask when you go inside."

Weston and I looked at one another in amazement. Wolfie barked toward Luigi, who was lounging in the afternoon sun, and toward Jackson who was munching some apples that he'd found in the grass.

What we heard was, "Hey Luigi, hey Jackson, come on over here."

Luigi and Jackson ran over to where Wolfie stood.

"Conway and Weston are going to pick some berries," he said to his two doggie friends. "Would you like to help them?"

"Oh, yeah! Oh, yeah! Oh, yeah! I'll help," said Jackson. His tail began wagging wildly. "I love blackberries."

"Jackson means he'll help you eat them," Wolfie explained. "He's not good at picking berries, but he's great at eating them—that is, if you're willing to share your berries with him."

Weston and I looked at each other and nodded. "Sure, we'll share."

"Me, too," said Luigi. "I like berries, too."

"You, too, Luigi?" Weston asked. Luigi wagged his tail.

I asked Wolfie, "How about you?"

"That's alright. I'm not a big berry eater. But Jackson and Luigi love them," Wolfie said. "I'll lie down in the shade of the bushes and keep everyone safe."

"Keep us safe?" I asked.

"Yes. That's my job. I'm the Guardian of Wutherwood."

"I don't know what that means."

"Well, your Grandmother named her home 'Wutherwood' long before I ever came to live with her. Everything you see—the house, the trees, the garden, the berry patch—she named it Wutherwood. And my job is to guard her and anyone else here. I must keep everyone safe. That's my job," Wolfie said

"Dogs have jobs?"

"Every dog has a job. My Chow Chow ancestors were palace guard dogs for the Emperor of China. I'm not in China, but protecting people is what I do. I'll protect everyone here as you pick your berries."

"May we eat some berries?" Weston asked.

"What's the magic word, Weston?" Conway asked.

"Please!" Weston said. "Let's go, Luigi!"

Weston and Luigi raced side-by-side to the berries.

As I walked with Wolfie and Jackson to the blackberry patch, Wolfie warned Weston. "Watch your fingers, Weston. Remember, berries bite."

I carefully picked a few plump, juicy berries and put them in my mouth. Jackson was sitting right next to me, I'm pretty sure he was smiling.

"May I have some berries, Conway?" Jackson was drooling in anticipation.

Wolfie looked at Jackson like a parent expecting something.

Jackson looked at Wolfie, and then he said, "Please!"

"Very good, Jackson. Very good," Wolfie said approvingly.

I smiled at Jackson, plucked a few more berries, and extended the palm of my hand toward Jackson. All those plump, ripe berries disappeared in the blink of an eye.

"Oh, those were yummy," Jackson said happily.

"I bet its Jackson's job to eat berries, isn't it?" I asked.

"Not exactly—but he is good at it. Jackson's job here is to entertain and comfort. If you want a dog to play fetch, Jackson's your guy. After all, fetching things—like a ball or a stick—that's what retrievers do. He's also a great snuggler. If you need a dog to snuggle up to for comfort, nobody's better than Jackson."

We looked over at Weston and Luigi who were having a great time eating berries together. Weston was smiling and giggling. He had purple berry juice running down his chin. Luigi happily licked his chin clean.

"How about Luigi?" I asked.

"Luigi is a loving companion. He's your Grandfather's dog. That also means your Grandfather is Luigi's human. As much as possible, they go everywhere together. When your Grandfather goes for a car ride, Luigi goes with him. When he watches television, Luigi lays down on his lap. When your Grandfather tucks in at night, Luigi scoots under the covers with him."

"Really? Luigi sleeps under the covers?" I asked.

"Yes, really, Conway. Luigi has very short hair, and when the nights are chilly he loves burrowing under the covers to stay warm."

"Yep. Luigi does what every dog is born to do."

"What's that?" I asked.

"Every dog is born to love a human being. To bring happiness into their lives even when terrible things happen—things that make humans unhappy.

A dog's job is to let their human know that whatever is happening, there is someone there to love them. Luigi provided love and comfort when your Grandfather's brother died. He did the same when your Grandfather's mother died. That's a dog's main job—to provide unconditional love."

I never knew that.

"And you came here to love Grandma and Grandpa?" I asked.

"Well, Conway, I'm a very lucky dog. I was rescued, and then your Grandma and Grandpa brought me here."

"So, are you the first dog here at Wutherwood?" I asked.

"Heavens, no. Lots of dogs have lived long, wonderful lives here. Of the three of us, Luigi was here first. Long before me. He was rescued by a kind man named Jimmy. In fact, we are all rescued dogs."

"I don't know what 'rescued' means," I said to Wolfie.

"It means that someone found us where we were—when we were lost or hurt. When we didn't have a forever home or an owner who treated us well. When things weren't very good for us. Our rescuers took us in, and then they found homes for us."

"Take Luigi. He was a lost dog—wandering the streets of a small town near Seattle. He didn't have a home. No dog should be without a home, Conway. Jimmy found Luigi and brought him to his home. Then he got in touch with your Grandmother. She adopted Luigi, and he's lived here ever since."

"And Jackson? Was he lost, too?" I asked.

"No, Jackson has a very different kind of challenge. As you can see, Jackson was born with only three paws. He was in a Texas dog shelter and the people looking after him were hoping that some kind person would adopt a three-legged dog and give him a home. A woman named Kelly, who works in dog-rescue, said she'd be happy to find Jackson a home."

"Didn't you say that Jackson was in Texas?" I asked. "Texas is really far away, isn't it?"

"Yes, it is. But Kelly had them put Jackson on an airplane and he flew all the way from Texas to Washington. Kelly met Jackson when his airplane landed in Seattle."

"Once Jackson was here, Kelly called your Grandmother," said

Wolfie, "and your Grandmother said she'd be pleased as punch to invite Jackson to live here. Now he's part of our pack."

Jackson howled happily. "Oh yeah! I had an airplane ride, Conway. They're lots of fun. I'm the only dog here that's ever had an airplane ride."

That's when I asked Wolfie, "You were rescued too, right? But you have all your paws. Were you lost like Luigi?"

"No. I was living in California when I ended up in the middle a terrible fight with other dogs. My owners took me to a veterinarian for my injuries, but then they abandoned me. Some humans are like that," Wolfie said sadly. "But only some owners. As it turns out, I had a guardian angel. A very kind woman named Annette rescued me, and she brought me to her home on Orcas Island here in Washington."

"And Grandma gave you a home?"

"Yes, she did," Wolfie said proudly. "Your Grandmother saw me on the internet and phoned Annette—the woman who rescued me—and your Grandmother and Grandfather took the ferry across Puget Sound to meet me on a beautiful sunshiny day just like today. They brought Luigi along to meet me, and I liked him right from the start."

I saw Wolfie smile. Then he said, "On that very same August day, they brought me here to live with them and Luigi. Any dog would be proud to call Wutherwood his forever home."

Weston and I spent two whole days climbing trees, eating berries, playing fetch, and talking with the dogs. Neither of us could get the cats to talk. Not one word. I'm not sure why.

So, I asked Grandma about the cats. "Wolfie talks a bunch," I said, "but I can't even get a word out of the cats."

Grandma just smiled. "Cats are particular, Conway," she said. "Try talking like a cat."

As we drove home, Mom and Dad asked us if we had a good time at Grandma and Grandpa's.

"You bet we did," we both said. "Can we go again? Please? That's the magic word, right?"

"Yes it is. We'll come back very soon, okay?"

Mom and Dad asked us what we had the most fun doing.

Weston said, "Eating berries."

I said, "Talking to the dogs. Especially Wolfie."

"That's nice," said Mom and Dad as we pulled into our driveway.

"Really," I said, "Dogs really do talk. Wolfie told us about how he was rescued—and how Luigi and Jackson were rescued, too. And he told us about the jobs each dog has."

Mom and Dad just smiled and said, "That's really nice, Conway. We're really happy that you both had a good time."

Wolfie was right about older humans. But dogs do talk. They really do. I know it, and now you know it, too. If you tell your Mom or Dad—and they don't believe you—well, that's okay. We know the truth. Just make sure you say "Hi" the next time you see a dog. Let me know if they say "Hi" back to you.

Mom asked me if I learned anything at Grandma's. I think I did. Those two days at Grandma and Grandpa's house helped me understand that dogs are just like people. They need love just like we do.

And best of all, if you let a dog into your home and into your heart, you'll always have someone who loves you. And someone you can talk to.

CPSIA information can be obtained
at www.ICGtesting.com
Printed in the USA
BVHW022204090721
611565BV00002B/21